How to Chair an Effective Meeting

 *effective meetings*
S E R I E S

How to Craft an Effective Agenda

How to Chair an Effective Meeting

How to Take Minutes Effectively

How to
Chair an Effective Meeting

Debi J. Peverill

Copyright ©2022 Debi J. Peverill

Published by Painless Financial Training Group Inc
5 Florence Street,
Lower Sackville, Nova Scotia
Canada B4J 1C5

Reproduction of this material in whole or in part without written authorization, by any duplication process whatsoever, both present and future, is a violation of copyright and offenders risk prosecution.

Disclaimer: Nothing in this book is intended to replace advice which is specific to your circumstances. This book is for educational purposes and is not professional advice.

ISBN: 978-1-989228-15-9 (paperback)
ISBN: 978-1-989228-16-6 (e-book)

How to Chair an Effective Meeting

Contents

Chapter 1: Importance of the Chair 1

Chapter 2: Behaviour at the Meeting...............3
  Meeting Rules... 3
  Behaviour of the Chair 6
  Dealing with Member Behaviour....................... 8
  Removal of Board Members............................13
  To Do 14

Chapter 3: Control of the Meeting — Agenda and Quorum 17
  Sticking to the Agenda................................ 18
  Allowing Additions to the Agenda 18
  Quorum 19
  To Do 21

Chapter 4: Motions................................... 23
  Making a Motion 23
  Motions to Accept Reports............................ 24
  Other Motions... 25
  Motions at Less-Formal Meetings 26
  To Do 27

Chapter 5: Virtual Meetings......................... 29
  Hosting the Virtual Meeting 30
  Video Function 30
  Chat Function..30
  Screen Sharing...31
  Speaking in Turn 32
  Leaving the Meeting 33
  Annotating on the Screen............................. 33
  Hybrid / Virtual Meetings..............................34
  To Do 35

Chapter 6: Board Decision-Making Framework 37
  ADAPPT 37
  A = Authority 38

D = Diligence 39
A = Accountability 39
P = Policies 40
P = Prudence 42
T = Transparency 42
To Do 43

Chapter 7: Voting Procedures 45
Voice Count 45
Show of Hands 46
Polls 47
Secret Ballots 47
Abstentions 48
Supermajority 49
Ties 50
To Do 51

Chapter 8: Running a Good Meeting 53

Chapter 9: Meeting Evaluations 57
Keeping Score 58
Evaluating the Chair 58
To Do 59

Glossary 61

Appendix A: Policies to Consider 65
Meeting Administration 65
Behaviour at the Meeting 66
Removal of Board Members 68
Control of the Meeting – Agenda and Quorum 69
Virtual Meetings 71

Appendix B: Consolidated List of Things to Do 75

Other Books by Debi J. Peverill 79

About the Author 81

For More Information 83

1 Importance of the Chair

Most meetings have a chair because someone has to be in charge. Maybe this person is you, and you picked up this book because you want to do a good job.

The chair fills a key role in the quest for an effective meeting by keeping order, enforcing the rules, and being fair.

Although there are many types of meetings – formal, informal, any meeting of more than two people benefits from having a chair. This is the person who takes care of the following:

- Creating and following the agenda
- Maintaining order
- Appointing a person to take minutes
- Making sure the minutes are distributed as appropriate

In a virtual meeting, the chair is probably the host and

controls who can speak, who can share their screen, and whether a participant is permitted to stay in the meeting.

The chair may be the boss, and if the boss is wise, they will gather all the information from other participants at the meeting before stating their opinion. This is assuming that the purpose of the meeting is to make a decision, and that the boss is looking for input.

Of course, there are different kinds of meetings. Perhaps the boss has called the meeting to tell the participants what to do. In that case, there is no need to hear from everyone.

If your meeting is a two-person meeting, you do not need a chair – but there should still be a stated goal, an agenda, and minutes or other notes kept. Otherwise, the meeting will not be effective.

If the meeting is worth having, then it is worth doing it right.

2 Behaviour at the Meeting

Meeting Rules

MEETING RULES WERE created to determine parliamentary procedures. *Bourinot's Rules of Order* are used in the parliament in Canada. *Robert's Rules of Order* are used in the parliament in the United States and are in more common use.

Your group may follow one of the official rules of order or you may establish rules for your own group. One version of *Robert's* is eight hundred pages long; some groups find that to be more than they need and develop a few simple rules of their own.

If you are having formal meetings, you need formal rules. A casual meeting may only need casual rules.

In any case, at the beginning of each meeting, the chair

should remind all the participants of the key rules in place for the meeting. This is particularly important when you have new participants, but it is the best practice for every meeting. People do require reminders of how they are supposed to behave. The chair is responsible for enforcing whatever rules are in place.

A group should have reference material that assists the group with their rules. The board binder is a collection of documents that make up the governance framework of the group. Information about the articles of incorporation, bylaws, memoranda of association, key agreements, past minutes, and the policies and procedures of the group are all items that could be contained in the board binder. The binder could be in a board-member-only area of the website, a Dropbox folder, or a Google doc. Wherever it is, the binder is where a board member could go to get information on the governance in place in the organization. This is particularly helpful for new board members.

If your group has not established any rules, you should consider doing just that. If your group has established a plan for meeting rules, you can skip this section.

These three rules are the minimum needed to have effective meetings:

1. *Only one person speaks at a time.*

This is the most important rule. Typically, the chair will keep track of who is allowed to speak – who "has the floor" in an in-person meeting, "has the screen" in a virtual meeting.

A participant will get the attention of the chair when they want to speak, usually by raising their hand, either in person or on a virtual call. The chair will nod at the participant who raised their hand and put their name on the list. When the current speaker is finished, the chair will refer to their list and let the next person know their time has come to talk. Maintaining order is key to an effective meeting, and the chair has that responsibility.

2. Only the chair can interrupt a speaker.

This is a rule that allows the first rule to work better. Participants know they will be allowed to finish explaining their points before anyone interrupts them. If a participant attempts to interrupt, the chair will let the interrupter know that is not allowed. The chair is the only one who can interrupt a participant.

The chair has the responsibility for making sure each participant feels comfortable enough to state their opinions. Also, the chair needs to stop participants who keep talking after they have finished stating their opinions. Participants may have to be encouraged to be succinct.

3. No personal attacks are allowed.

Word this rule however you like, but be sure your participants are aware they need to discuss the issues – not complain about personalities or indicate their fellow participants are fools.

Your group may have many more rules about meeting behaviour, for example, about whether the chair can vote.

Behaviour of the Chair

The tone of any meeting is set by the chair. An effective meeting will not happen without an effective chair. If the meeting is chaotic, with participants calling each other names or people storming out of the meeting, it is the chair who is to blame.

Another book in this series, *How to Craft an Effective Agenda*, talks about setting a goal for the meeting. More information is available there, but in summary: Do not call a meeting unless you know what you are trying to accomplish at the meeting. Write down the goal, and an effective chair will make sure the goal is achieved.

Contributions of the Chair

Opinions vary, but in general the chair should not be contributing their opinion until all others have been heard from. The chair's role is to facilitate the discussion and get the most out of the participants. The chair in most cases does not even have a vote.

Being the chair can make some people feel they are

important, but chairing a meeting is not about telling everyone else what to think. Expressing an opinion may be necessary if there is a tie vote and the chair has to cast the deciding vote; otherwise, the opinion of the chair may not be necessary.

A skillful chair calls on the least senior person at the meeting first. If a very senior person talks first, everyone else may rush to agree with them. Everyone wants the best ideas for the organization; you want to hear from everyone without fear of disagreeing with the boss.

Again, remember the chair is there to facilitate the meeting, to get the best decisions by having all the participants contribute to making the decision.

Equal Opportunities, or Don't Play Favourites

The chair must treat everyone in the same manner. Consistency is important if participants are going to respect the chair.

Rules apply to everyone.

The participants should be permitted to speak in the order they request the floor. The chair acknowledges participants who indicate they have something to say and keeps a list of names in order. It is not appropriate to put a participant ahead of another, out of the order they made the request.

End on Time

How important is it to the group to end on time? Fairly important. Participants have other places to be, so if the ending time arrives and the meeting has not ended, some participants may leave even though the agenda has not been completed.

If the group has been unable to get through the agenda, then either the meeting must continue (if the meeting still has quorum), or the rest of the items on the agenda must be tabled and be discussed at the next meeting.

Either of these outcomes is the responsibility of the chair. The chair should decide whether the problem is with the agenda or the management of the meeting. Either problem needs to be fixed.

Policy Enforcement

The chair will have to remind people about the policies set by the board and enforce them.

Dealing with Member Behaviour

Participants need to be told how to behave at a meeting. It is not wise to assume they know the proper behaviour. The chair should make sure that the participants know about policies that deal with the tone of the meeting and respectful behaviour.

The chair should know how to deal with the following:

members who interrupt, talk too long, are reluctant to speak, arrive late, fail to prepare for the meeting, or are disrespectful.

Being polite but firm is a skill a board chair needs to develop.

Members Who Interrupt

If a board member interrupts another member at the meeting, the chair stops the interruption and makes sure the policies are being followed.

The chair could say, "Excuse me John, Phyllis has the floor; we will let her finish before anyone else speaks. Phyllis, please continue."

Hopefully, John apologizes and does not interrupt anyone else for the rest of the meeting.

The board chair must do this every time there is an interruption. Policies that are not enforced will never be followed.

Members Who Talk Too Long

If a participant is rambling on and repeating themselves, the chair must gently fix this as well. "Excuse me Phyllis, I think you have made this point already. Is there anything else you would like to say or should we give John a chance to speak?"

Members Who Are Reluctant to Speak

The goal of many meetings is to make a decision after hearing from everyone who was invited to the meeting. If you want to hear from everyone, the chair must make sure participants are comfortable in voicing their opinion.

There may be participants who are reluctant to speak no matter what they have been told. If some people seem to be unwilling to comment or express their views, the chair is going to have to ask them. The chair should keep a list of the participants and place a tick beside a participant's name every time they talk. Occasionally, the chair should look at this list and call on those participants with the least number of ticks beside their names.

The purpose of a board is to get input from everyone who serves on the board. A board chair will ask everyone if they have anything else to add to the conversation before asking for the vote and moving on.

Equal participation is a delicate balance. You want the meeting to move along with everyone saying something; you do not want the meeting to be endless.

Members Who Arrive Late

It is frustrating for members who arrive on time to wait for the meeting to start because others are late.

Your policies should indicate meetings start at the appointed time. You might also have a policy that after a certain time has elapsed latecomers may not be granted entry. This is easy to do on a virtual call: you enable the waiting room and don't let anyone in after the ten-minute mark. Harder to do in person, but a locked door can work. Maybe even a sign on the door that a meeting is in progress, and no one can enter.

If the group has allowed people to wander in late to meetings, then before the policy can be changed, people will have to agree on the change and be reminded a few times that the policy has changed.

Remember, a latecomer is disruptive to the meeting: they arrive as a discussion is taking place and take time to find a seat and sort out their papers, they ask about matters that have already been discussed, and they may not have muted themselves.

Members Who Fail to Prepare for the Meetings

Participants who fail to prepare properly for meetings need to be reminded to read all the material sent before the meeting. The chair may have to contact the participant in private and remind them of the requirement and find out why the preparation is not taking place. This must be done in a respectful manner, not during a meeting, particularly if the member is a volunteer. A little one-on-one coaching goes a long way toward resolving these issues.

Members Who Are Disrespectful

The purpose of the meeting should be clear. Participants are there to talk about the issues. The chair is there to make sure this happens. The chair needs to stop conversations starting like this, "You are wrong and you are a fool." The issue of who is a fool is not relevant to this discussion. That might be relevant to whether someone is worthy of being on the board to begin with, but that is not likely to be the subject of this meeting.

Board members will need training if they are not used to separating the issues from the personalities. This type of reaction has become more common in politics, but the rest of us should aspire to better behaviour. The behaviour that is best for the meeting is to find out why the person feels the way they do.

Here's an example of some correct and incorrect ways to respond:

> Joanne says, "I don't think we should be asking our members to wear masks at our gatherings."
>
> Sally says, "Why do you think that?"
> **= correct response**
>
> Beth says "Are you one of those anti-vaccine nuts?"
> **= *incorrect response***
>
> Joanne replies to Sally, "I believe that personal freedoms are the cornerstone of our democracy, and we should not be taking these freedoms away."
> **= correct response to the correct response**

Joanne replies to Beth, "I am not a nut; you are a fascist." = ***incorrect response to the incorrect response***

This conversation could spiral out of control with no real discussion taking place.

Part of respectful meeting training is to help participants understand that it is possible for someone to disagree without getting their feelings hurt. A disagreement should not be interpreted as a personal attack. Groups can work together even when they disagree about some of the issues. Agreement can be reached. Each board member has a duty to do what is best for the organization, which includes having an open mind and being willing to work with people who hold different viewpoints.

In fact, if a group's members are always in perfect agreement, some of them are not doing any critical thinking. It is improbable that everyone at a meeting agrees with all the decisions being made. Unless the meeting is just to agree with the boss, participants should have different points of view and be able to express them.

Removal of Board Members

Sometimes a participant will not behave, and the chair must remove the participant from the meeting. The chair has the authority to do this. This is easy to do in a virtual meeting as it can be done with the click of a mouse. Asking a board member to leave an in-person meeting is a more difficult task.

A member who misbehaves at more than one meeting should be asked to leave the board or the group. However, removing a person from the group is a more permanent solution. The chair may not have the authority for this, and it is probably a task for the full board or a discipline subcommittee.

The circumstances in which a member can be removed should be laid out by policy. For example, if a participant is warned twice by the chair about aspects of their behaviour, and the behaviour does not change – a committee will investigate the situation. If it is true that the participant has been warned twice and has not changed their behaviour, the committee can apply the policy and ask the participant to leave the board.

Each group will have their own committees. There may not be a discipline committee, so the nominating committee might include discipline in their terms of reference. It will depend on how often disciplining members is required.

To Do

- ✓ Choose which official rules of order you will use to run your meetings.

- ✓ Write up the key meeting rules that you will remind the participants of at each meeting.
- ✓ Decide on the goal of every meeting.
- ✓ Create a policy on whether the chair votes.
- ✓ Create policies on what to do when participants are not respectful or are late.
- ✓ Create a policy on how to remove a member from a meeting or from the organization.

3 Control of the Meeting — Agenda and Quorum

THE CHAIR IS responsible for the pacing of the meeting. If the agenda was properly designed, it is a road map for the meeting. There should only be as many items on the agenda as can be dealt with in the time allotted for the meeting. Participants are grateful when a meeting starts and ends on time. A part of making that happen is controlling the agenda, both in how it is created and protecting it during the meeting. See the book in this series, *Effective Meetings: How to Craft an Effective Agenda*, for more information.

The challenge for the meeting chair is to avoid distractions and keep the meeting moving along.

Sticking to the Agenda

Sometimes the discussion of an agenda item gets off track, and the group starts talking about a topic that is not on the agenda. This can happen by accident.

In this case, the chair points out that the item is not on the agenda and should be parked. To park something means to keep a list of topics that come up during the meeting that need to be added to a future agenda. The person taking the minutes maintains the list of parked items, and the chair uses this list when drafting the agenda for the next meeting.

Or, it could be a participant wants an item discussed at the meeting that wasn't on the agenda; the participant is attempting an end run around the agenda process. In this case, the participant is being a nuisance, and the chair needs to deal with the conversation firmly. The chair should say, "We are drifting into a discussion of something that is not on the agenda. This discussion is not appropriate, and we will get back on track and discuss what is on the agenda."

Allowing Additions to the Agenda

Each group should establish a policy for additions to the agenda. I recommend that the agenda be prepared ahead of the meeting and that no additions be allowed during the meeting.

If participants ignore that process and simply show up at the meeting with thoughts on what should be discussed, they are not following the policy. The chair then reminds everyone of the policy. If the board chair allows additions to the agenda at the meeting, then no one will look at the agenda until the meeting.

Does your policy allow for emergency additions to the agenda? If so, the emergency should be both time sensitive and crucial. Clearly it is best if this is established by policy. The participants can vote on whether they think the proposed agenda addition meets the emergency agenda addition policy. If the participants vote in favour, then the item will be added to the agenda.

Items that are not emergencies are not added to the agenda. They are parked.

An emergency addition to the agenda should be a rare event. Hopefully, the organization is not experiencing so much drama that there is an emergency addition to the agenda every month. If so, the chair should look at the structure of the organization and the policies to determine the cause.

Quorum

Quorum is the minimum number of people who need to be present at a meeting so the decisions made will be legal.

If you need quorum and you don't have one, the start of a meeting must be delayed. Not every meeting is so formal that there is a quorum requirement. But if it is a board meeting, quorum is crucial. Without quorum, you cannot pass any motions, and the meeting might not be able to proceed. If a meeting does not have quorum, you need to decide: Do you wait for latecomers or do you adjourn the meeting without accomplishing anything?

How to Make Sure You Have Quorum

There are a few procedures you can implement to improve your chances of having quorum. If your meetings are always held at the same time, such as the first Wednesday of each month, your participants can work this into their schedule. If the meeting is important to a participant, they will keep their schedule clear at the time of the meeting. If the meeting times are set a few meetings at a time, the participants are able to block the time out of their schedule. If the meetings are held at random times, attendance can be more of an issue.

Reminders and confirmations are useful in getting participants to the meeting. About a week before a meeting – or at the time the agenda is being circulated – the chair should send a notice reminding the board members about the meeting. Ask the participants to confirm whether they are attending or not. This notice improves the chance of attendance because the participants will have been reminded about the meeting, and it reminds participants to confirm attendance.

If a few participants indicate they are unable to attend, the chair might have to cancel the meeting.

A consistent problem with quorum is an indication of larger issues with your group. If the participants are not making attendance a priority, the chair needs to take action.

Can you find people who are more committed to the goals of the group? Or is there a problem with the direction the organization is taking – and the board members are losing their interest. Or are the meetings not effective, so participants do not want to attend. A problem with quorum becomes the chair's responsibility.

To Do

- ✓ Create a policy for when additions to the agenda are allowed under both normal and emergency conditions.

- ✓ Make sure you know what quorum has been established for your organization.

- ✓ Send reminders for meetings and ask for confirmation of attendance to ensure quorum at meetings.

4 Motions

THE BOARD CHAIR needs to keep track of the motions on the table and make sure the rules of the meeting are being followed.

The decisions made at a meeting are recorded in the form of motions. Less-formal meetings do not have motions.

Making a Motion

A policy should be established for how a participant gets the attention of the chair. A common way for a participant to make the chair aware they want to speak next is to raise their hand. The chair will nod at the person who has raised their hand to indicate they have seen the raised hand, keep a list of people wishing to speak, and call on them in order.

There is only one motion on the table at a time. This is

the chair's responsibility. If someone is attempting to make a motion, and the previous motion has not been resolved, the chair should point out there is already a motion on the table.

The chair stops the meeting until the original motion is dealt with. Either the chair calls for a vote on the motion, or the original mover withdraws the motion. Once this motion has been dealt with, you can move on to the next motion.

Motions to Accept Reports

At the end of each report, after the person making the report has answered any questions, it is common for the chair to call for a motion to accept this report.

For example, the treasurer has presented the year-to-date financial statements and answered a couple of questions. She might say, "Are there any further questions?"

If she hears none, the chair will say, "Could we have a motion to accept?"

The treasurer might say, "I move that we accept the financial statements for the five-month period ended May 31, as presented, subject to the annual audit."

Someone must second the motion, then the board votes, and the motion is either carried or defeated.

It would be rare for a motion to accept a report to fail.

This usually only happens when the participants still have questions.

Other Motions

Calling the Question

Some participants may feel the chair is moving too slowly with the discussion. It is usually the chair who says, "We have now heard from everyone, are we ready to make a motion and move on?" or "Would someone like to make the motion?" Once this happens, the discussion is over, and the voting can begin.

However, there are participants who want to move on before this and end the debate immediately. A participant could get the attention of the chair and then say, "I call the question." This motion must be seconded and voted on. If passed it means the debate is over for the motion that was on the table, and it must be voted on immediately.

Point of Order

A participant can interrupt the meeting with a point of order. The participant could say, "Point of order, Chair."

After the chair acknowledges the participant, the person states their point. This is typically something has not happened that should have. Perhaps the meeting has not been called to order, but someone is attempting to do some business. Or a motion is being made, but a previous motion has not been voted on. Or maybe there is no quorum.

A point of order usually means the chair has missed something that should have been dealt with.

Point of Privilege

A participant may also interrupt due to a point of privilege. A point of privilege occurs when a participant cannot hear the speaker, for example, or finds the room either too hot or too cold. These are items that should be addressed immediately.

Motions at Less-Formal Meetings

Your group may not want to say the words, "Point of Order, Madam Speaker," or the even more formal, "I rise on a point of privilege, Madam Speaker." If this is the case, you can set the same rules without using the formal names.

No matter whether you have formal or informal meetings, participants should be able to speak without interruption; however, you do want a person to be able to interrupt to indicate that they cannot hear!

To Do

✓ Keep track of motions on the floor; make sure the meeting rules are being followed.

✓ Create a policy for how participants get the attention of the chair.

✓ Keep track of people who would like to speak and call them in order.

5 Virtual Meetings

VIRTUAL MEETINGS PRESENT challenges and opportunities for both chairs and participants. Meetings can occur more frequently because geography is not a constraint, but the challenge is to keep the participants engaged.

When you have participants in a room, you can tell whether they are checking their email on their phones or have fallen asleep. When your participants are joining virtually, it is more difficult to see whether they are engaged.

Sometimes the chair can insist that participants turn their cameras on. For many participants, looking at a screen full of black boxes with white names does not feel like a meeting. Seeing the actual faces of the participants will help make the experience feel more like a meeting.

Hosting the Virtual Meeting

The chair should be the host of the meeting or at least the co-host. This will give the chair the ability to mute and unmute participants, to enable the waiting room, and – in extreme cases – to kick participants out of the meeting. The chair can also enable screen sharing for participants or not.

Video Function

With the cameras turned on, the chair will get more information about the participants in the meeting. Are they smiling? Puzzled? Paying attention?

With the cameras turned off, the participants can do other stuff while the meeting goes on: make faces, eat lunch, pay attention to other tasks, and so forth. In general, participants are less engaged in the actual meeting.

For meetings that are presentations, where participants can zone in and out, then cameras off makes sense. For board meetings, where participants need to have high engagement, then cameras on is better.

Chat Function

In a virtual meeting, there are two streams of activity happening at the same time: the screen and the chat.

The chair must pay attention to both, which can be a challenge on occasion.

Sometimes it is helpful to have another person monitor the chat, especially if they are not a participant. This is more important with larger meetings. The chat can be quite active and the chair may have a hard time keeping their train of thought when the chat is streaming by.

Some of the same rules apply to the chat. You are not allowed to call someone a fool in the chat, any more than you can do so when you have the screen.

The chair may decide the chat function should be turned off during some meetings to keep the group focused. It is a challenge to keep focus on a virtual meeting as it is, and the chat can add to the distraction; of course, the chat increases engagement, so there is a trade-off.

Screen Sharing

In a virtual meeting, rather than handing out paper, participants can share their screens with each other. Remember, anything that participants needed to read and think about should have been sent out before the meeting. Since this was probably done electronically, that digital package of materials can be displayed on the screen as the meeting progresses.

Do you want participants to be able to share their

screens? Generally, the answer should be yes, unless you are having trouble with participants not being respectful.

If the chair has set the virtual meeting to have a password, then people who are not a part of the group do not have access to the meeting. Zoom has taken extra steps to avoid unwanted participants, as, during the early days of the pandemic, some well-publicized "Zoom bombings" occurred. The chair has two methods to deny non-members access the meeting: have a password for the meeting and enable the waiting room.

Caution participants to use their own names when they register for an online videoconferencing software account. If the participants use an alias, then they might not gain access to some meetings as the host might not recognize the name.

Speaking in Turn

Occasionally participants will talk over each other because of a lag in the audio. That can only be helped with better technology. However, a board chair can change the setting so that participants cannot unmute themselves; only the host of the meeting can unmute. This gives the chair more control than they have at an in-person meeting.

Participants can use the chat function to indicate they would like to speak next, or use the raise-hand button. The chair will keep track of this in the same way they do when participants are all around the same table: keep a list in order of request.

Leaving the Meeting

Participants can leave the meeting whenever they like, and chairs can remove participants from a meeting. If participant is unruly, the chair can remove them with a couple of clicks. This is far easier than the in-person scenario in which you must call security or the police to remove a participant.

If the chair removes a participant and the waiting room is enabled, the unruly participant will not be able to get back into the meeting without the chair's permission.

Annotating on the Screen

The annotate function – the ability to write on the screen – is quite useful for improving the interaction of the group. It can encourage participation. Polls do the same thing but must be set up each time (and often ahead of time), whereas a slide on your power point can be used over and over again.

The chair can use the annotation function for brainstorming as well. Participants can use the text tool to write on the screen as they would a white board.

The chair has control over clearing any annotations; as

long as they act quickly when something inappropriate shows up, there is probably no need for annotation to be restricted.

Hybrid / Virtual Meetings

A hybrid meeting has additional challenges. Some participants are in a meeting room, and some are virtual. If this is a workplace meeting, you could have a policy that all people are to use their computers rather than having some people in a conference room and some people remotely on their machines. This will make the communication the same for everyone, rather than better for the people in the room. The people in the room have other methods for communicating, they could be whispering among themselves with the audio off.

Of course, your group will make their own policy about this. If only one person is coming in remotely, the policy of everyone being in their own offices might not be the best choice.

No matter how the participants are attending the meeting, the chair must make an effort to include everyone.

A chair has to be pretty skillful to deal with hybrid meetings – to make sure everyone participates, and no one feels like they have been excluded.

To Do

✓ Create policies for the use of video, chat, screen sharing, and annotation in a virtual meeting.

✓ Create a policy about how hybrid meetings will work.

6 Board Decision-Making Framework

ONE OF THE roles of the board chair in conducting the meeting is to ensure that the participants satisfy their responsibilities to the organization.

The board must demonstrate due diligence in making decisions and must document the process for this decision making. It is the chair's responsibility to make this happen at each meeting.

ADAPPT

Years ago, I developed a framework for boards to follow when making decisions. This framework is designed to help boards satisfy their duty of care and thus stay out of trouble. The duty of care requires board members to behave in an ethical manner with a view to the best interests of the organization. This framework works for any decision. The framework has the following aspects:

A = authority
D = diligence
A = accountability
P = policy
P = prudence
T = transparency

A = Authority

This is the first step in the decision-making process. If you do not have the authority to make the decision, then you do not need to deal with the rest of the framework, because you are not going to be making the decision.

Examples of boards having no authority occurred during the pandemic. All over the world, health departments told businesses and non-profits that they could not open for business, limited the number of people who could be in the premises, and mandated cleaning protocols and mask wearing. Organizations did not have the authority to open or meet because of the national or provincial health departments.

In these situations, the group is not making decisions, they are following the rules set by others.

The first step toward any decision being made at a group meeting is to determine whether the board does, in fact, have the authority to make the decision or not.

D = Diligence

Assuming the group can make the decision, the next step is to determine whether they have all the information they need to make an informed decision. Do they have all the facts they would like to have? Are there experts they would like to hear from, to help them make the decision?

The need for diligence means last-minute additions to the agenda are not a good idea. Making decisions in a hurry is not the best practice. Better decisions are made when the group has all the facts and time to consider all facets of a decision.

A = Accountability

Is the group ready to accept the responsibility for making this decision? Typically, this occurs when the group has all the information they need and have considered it carefully. They are ready to move on to the next steps on the framework.

Sometimes a participant will ask for more time to consider this decision. Others may agree that they would also like more time. The decision is then "tabled" until the next meeting.

The board could also decide to refer the decision to a committee, or back to management, for further analysis.

This step of the decision-making process is not over until the board is ready to move on.

P = Policies

Policies help to make decisions consistent and save the board time.

- Do you have a policy about this decision?
- Should you have a policy about this decision?
- Do you have a policy that you do not want to follow?

Do You Have a Policy?

The chair can simply remind the board of the policy when a topic arises at a board meeting and the board already has a policy on the topic. You don't need to discuss the item again. The decision has effectively been made, provided you are comfortable following the policy.

Should You Have a Policy?

Is this the type of decision you might make again? Has this come up before? Board time is precious, so if this is a decision that might come up more than once, setting a policy will be a time saver and will help future iterations of the board.

Having a policy will also lead to the decisions being

made more consistently – always an improvement in meeting performance.

Do You Have a Policy That You Do Not Want to Follow?

Sometimes, the group has a policy but is reluctant to apply it. The duty of care requires members act in the best interest of the organization. Making a decision against their own policies is a tough one to defend.

First decide whether the policy in existence needs to be changed. Perhaps the policy was set a long time ago?

If the policy still seems relevant but the group does not want to follow it – figure out why. Is this situation a logical exception to the policy or is the group being illogical? For example, you may have a policy that you don't want to apply because it involves a friend of the board. This, of course, is wrong.

If you follow tennis, you may have seen Novak Djokovic being ejected from the US Open because he hit an official with a ball. The policy is clear and applies to everyone, but you can see the temptation. Novak was the number one seed, and forcing him to leave the tournament would reduce the number of viewers. Congratulations to the officials for correctly applying the policy, no matter who was involved.

P = Prudence

This only applies to not-for-profit situations. A not-for-profit board must use prudence when making decisions because they are not dealing with their own money. Particularly if the organization has government funding, a board must be fiscally responsible.

A business is not required to be prudent, especially if all the board members are also shareholders. The group can decide whether prudence should be a part of their framework or not.

T = Transparency

One of the principles of good governance is transparency, that is, the board must be able to explain how and why decisions are made.

For example, the board is hiring a new executive director:

> They have an application form and a list of desirable qualities and characteristics.
>
> They advertise this position on both social media and conventional channels.
>
> A committee is struck to evaluate all the applications received and to score them on the qualities the board is looking for.
>
> The top ten highest-scoring candidates are

interviewed by the committee, and the number of candidates is reduced to five.

The five are interviewed again, and the list is further reduced to two.

The full board interviews the final two and makes the decision about who will be hired.

The board announces the candidate who is hired.

In recording the minutes of the meeting where the candidate was hired, only the name would be in the minutes and the synopsis of the process followed.

This is a transparent process. If necessary, the application form and the list of qualities and qualifications can be shown to anyone who asks.

Actions that must not happen:

The board releases the names of the applicants who were not successful.

The board releases all the scores of the candidates.

To Do

✓ Create a policy for ensuring the summary of any discussion shows that the group demonstrated diligence, followed existing policy, and was transparent.

7 Voting Procedures

Each meeting has goals and decisions that need to be made. These decisions need to be recorded in some way. Voting is the typical method. The chair can use various methods to ask for and record a vote on a motion. Ayes, nays, and abstentions can be counted in the following ways:

- Voice count
- Show of hands
- Secret ballot
- Polls

Voice Count

Most commonly the chair asks for a vote, "We have a motion on the floor. All those in favour of this motion please signify by saying aye."

At this point, some people will say aye. The chair then says, "Contrary minded, if any, signify by saying nay." Perhaps no one says "nay," in which case, the minutes will show the motion was passed unanimously.

If there are nays, it may not be clear whether the motion has enough votes to pass. A voice count only works when the vote is not close. If the vote is close, it can be hard to hear whether there are more ayes than nays. In this case, the chair will increase the certainty of the vote by moving to a show of hands.

Show of Hands

Voting with a show of hands will be more conclusive. The chair asks for all in favour to raise their hands. The chair can then count the number of people with their hands in the air to determine whether there is a majority. If the motion is being passed by a simple majority, then the chair will declare the motion passed or defeated depending on the show of hands. If there are twelve people on the board and eight vote in favour, then the chair will declare the motion passed. If there is a tie, then the bylaws of the organization will have to be consulted. In some cases, a tie is broken by the chair exercising a vote. In other situations, a tie means the motion is defeated. More on ties later.

Your group may also allow abstentions, which will complicate the counting, more on abstentions later.

Polls

Polling can happen in either in-person meetings or when using virtual meeting software.

In online meetings, the chair sets up a poll for each vote ahead of time as a list of questions that the participants can answer. If the polls are set up as motions, then the polling function can be used for passing these motions.

In in-person polls, the chair asks each participant to state how they vote on a motion. The chair will make a note of the vote and once everyone has been asked, the chair will conclude whether the vote has passed. This type of voting is stressful when the matter being decided is controversial. Shy participants may be afraid to state their opinion in front of everyone else. Some participants, who are not shy, might ask for polling to intimidate others into voting with them.

An example of in-person polling is at a trial by jury. Each member of the jury is asked to state whether they find the defendant guilty or not guilty.

Secret Ballots

Secret ballots can be more relaxing than polling in person. Unless the vote is unanimous, no one will know how each participant voted. Our parliamentary system works this way. Each voter is given privacy to mark their ballot in an election.

A vote may be held by secret ballot if the chair is concerned that participants are feeling intimidated by others.

At in-person meetings, the chair hands out pieces of paper and something to collect the ballots. The chair or the secretary will count the ballots once they are all collected. No one will know who put which ballot in or how a person's ballot was marked.

At online meetings, the chair can set up polls and ask each participant to respond anonymously.

This method of voting is appropriate for contentious issues. Some issues can be difficult to decide upon, and some participants may be lobbying others. If participants appear nervous about casting their vote because others might judge them, the chair needs to take the necessary steps to allow people to feel comfortable in voting. The secret ballot will accomplish this.

Of course, if the vote is ten to one, the person who cast the negative vote will know everyone else voted differently. The others will not be sure who cast the negative vote.

Abstentions

What about the person who does not want to vote? Abstentions are rarely necessary. Participants are at the meeting to express their opinion.

If a participant abstains because they do not understand the issue, then the chair should get them the information they need and facilitate more discussion.

If a participant has a conflict of interest with the matters being discussed at this meeting, they should not be at this part of the meeting. There is no need for them to abstain, because the chair has moved them to a breakout room (if the meeting is virtual), or the chair has asked them to step out of the room (if the meeting is held in person).

Some people attending the meeting do not have a vote, so they don't vote. They are not abstaining; they simply do not have a vote to cast. For example, guests do not have a vote.

Sometimes, votes that are ineligible are called abstentions. For example, a participant who was not in attendance at the previous meeting cannot vote to approve the minutes. I suggest they are not eligible, but abstaining is often the word used.

Supermajority

A supermajority means that more than the usual number of the attendees must agree to a change.

Some issues – for example, bylaw changes – must be decided by more than a simple majority. A simple majority is 50 percent or more. For a supermajority, 75 percent is the usual percentage of positive votes required. Your group could choose a different number, that is, you could determine that two-thirds of the attendees voting positively can pass a vote.

The chair must take the time to research these matters and become aware of the percentages needed for the supermajority and the situations in which it would apply.

Ties

What if there are eight participants and the vote is four to four? In some groups, the chair casts the deciding vote. In other groups, a tie means the motion has not been approved; a tie is taken as a negative vote and the motion fails.

Your group might decide that when the participants are evenly split on an issue, it requires more time for consideration. Perhaps you suggest the motion be tabled and discussed at the next meeting. This would be an appropriate choice if you think more time and more information might help to unite the group. Is there some other expert or some other piece of information that would help with this decision-making process?

It is also possible more time will not help, as the group is divided and may be unwilling to reconsider their opinion. It's better to have participants who are able to change their minds when they hear new information. The chair now has some work to do in assisting participants to reach the decision that is best for the organization.

To Do

- ✓ Determine the best method for voting on each issue.

- ✓ Determine what percentage of positive votes is needed for a supermajority and ensure that the conditions requiring a supermajority are known to the board.

- ✓ Create a policy on what should be done in the case of a tie vote.

8 Running a Good Meeting

Here is a short summary of how to run a good meeting.

Start the meeting on time – Starting a meeting on time is easy unless you do not have quorum. If you start a meeting on time, every time, participants will stop showing up late.

End a meeting on time – Craft the agenda properly and keep the conversation on track. Running a meeting such that all the items on the agenda are covered and the meeting ends on time takes practice. If the policy is to have the meetings last no longer than two hours and the agenda is longer than that, then lengthen the meetings or have them more frequently.

Make sure you have quorum – Schedule the meetings ahead of time, remind the participants frequently, expect all members to attend all the meetings, and remove any members who fail to attend. Have a staff member confirm attendance with the participants a few days before the meeting. If the meeting is virtual, then send an email with the meeting link and password an hour before the meeting. This one step will avoid the problem of participants who are ready to attend but can't find how to sign in.

Declare a goal for the meeting – Every meeting should have a goal, and all the participants should know the goal. It also helps if the only way to accomplish the goal is to have the meeting. If the goal could be accomplished with an email, don't expect good attendance at a meeting.

Ensure participant engagement – Did every participant contribute to the conversation? If not, the chair should make a point of asking the participant what they think. The chair should track conversations and ask the shyer participants to speak. If you have participants who don't have an opinion, even if asked, then these people are not well-suited to being at the meeting.

Keep to the point – The chair should keep participants on track when they are talking. Do not allow additional items to be discussed and do keep the conversations focused. If there are participants who have a lot of trouble coming to the point, the chair should be gentle but firm about the conversation staying on track. Sometimes the chair needs to have a private conversation with a participant to explain this policy.

Keep the meeting respectful – Interrupt people and

stop them from talking when they are being disrespectful. Remind them of the policies.

Train the participants – Explain policies and procedures to them. Perhaps a meeting could be scheduled just for that purpose. There should be some training material that participants can look at on their own. Or, the chair can remind participants at the start of the meeting about the rules.

Train new members – New board members may be experienced in board governance or they may not. The chair will coordinate with the nominating committee to see what training may be needed and to support the new board member in getting the information they need to become familiar with the organization. The new members will be given access to a copy of the board binder, which contains all the documents of the governance framework of the group.

9 Meeting Evaluations

To have effective meetings, each meeting needs to be evaluated. Here are some questions to ask:

- Did the meeting start on time?
- Did the meeting end on time?
- Did we follow the agenda?
- Did we have quorum?
- Did we accomplish the goal of the meeting?
- Did we know the goal of the meeting when it started?
- Did everyone participate in the meeting?
- Were all the conversations respectful?
- Were all the conversations focused on the issues being discussed?
- Is there anything else that could improve the meeting?

You can shorten this list of questions or add some of your own.

Keeping Score

Keep track of the score you get when you answer these questions. This enables you to watch the trends over time. Is the effectiveness score improving or not? Do you see the same issues coming up over an over? If so, the chair should intervene and make the necessary changes. Of course, the problem could be the chair.

Evaluating the Chair

The effectiveness of the meeting reflects on the chair. Most of the questions are about items that are under the control of the chair. Therefore, the meeting evaluation needs to be done somewhat anonymously. Participants need to be able to answer questions in a truthful manner without having the chair react badly.

For a board, the nomination committee is responsible for evaluating the chair. The nominating committee is responsible for finding and training board members and board chairs. It is part of their mandate to monitor performance of the board. These are the people to gather the meeting evaluations and have a private chat with the chair about any areas of trouble.

To Do

✓ Set up a way to evaluate the meetings. Determine the questions that need to be asked. Set up a way to keep score over time.

✓ Ensure that the board has a way to evaluate the chair.

Glossary

Adjourn – the end of a meeting. Someone makes a motion to adjourn and, at that time, the meeting is over.

Agenda – a plan for the meeting. The agenda could be a standard listing of all the items to be discussed at a board meeting, which will be the same each time. An agenda could be a list of the decisions to be made.

Board – a short form of "board of directors," "board of governors," and so forth. A board is elected by the members at the annual general meeting to oversee the running of the organization.

Board Binder – a collection of documents that make up the governance framework of the group. Information about the articles of incorporation, bylaws, memoranda of association, key agreements, past minutes, and the policies and procedures of the group are all items that could be contained in the board binder.

Chair or chairperson – the person at the meeting who leads the discussion and is responsible for keeping the meeting on schedule and compliant with the rules.

Chat – the ability to type comments into a section of the screen during a virtual meeting. This ability can be turned on or off by the host.

Committee – a group with a specific task who meets and reports to the board. Typical examples are the audit committee, finance committee, and human resource committee.

Guest – a person who is invited to a meeting. They do not have a vote but are allowed to make comments. A guest can be at meeting for a specific period of time to discuss some issue. For example, a lawyer might come to a meeting to talk about potential litigation.

Majority – the percentage of the participants who must vote in favour of a motion for it to be approved. This figure is usually more than 50 percent of the participants.

Meeting – a group of people (more than one) gathering to make decisions. The meeting can be as formal as the board meeting of a corporation or as casual as two people deciding about lunch.

Member – a person who has privileges because of joining an organization.

Minutes – the record of what was accomplished at the meeting. This can be a written record or audio and video recordings.

Motion – a series of conversations at a meeting that result in a decision being voted on by the group. For example, John says, "I move to approve the agenda." The chair says, "Do I have a seconder?" Sally says, "I second that motion." The chair says, "All those in favour signify by saying "aye." Everyone says aye, and the motion is passed, which means that the agenda has been approved. A motion may also be called a resolution.

Motion passed – a motion gets enough votes in favour. For example, a motion to adjourn the meeting has passed if a majority of the participants vote to adjourn.

Motion defeated – a motion fails to get enough votes. This means that whatever was being moved is not going to happen.

Motion tabled – the group decides they are not going to decide on the issue at this meeting. The working phrase is "We will table this motion until the next meeting." Typically, this is done when the group wants more time to make the decision.

Park/Parking Lot – when an issue raised at a meeting is placed on a list to be considered for inclusion in a future agenda.

Participant – a person attending a meeting who can vote.

Point of order – a formal method for a participant to interrupt the person speaking without breaking the rules. Typically, a point of order is invoked when a participant feels that something is being done incorrectly. For example, if a person has made a motion but the previous motion has not been voted on, a new motion cannot be made, and a participant may call a point of order.

Point of privilege – a way of interrupting the person speaking without breaking the rules. This may occur because the participant cannot hear the speaker, or they are too cold, too hot, or too something. This is more of a personal point than the point of order and is sometimes called a point of personal privilege.

Quorum – the minimum number of participants required to be in attendance at a meeting before the meeting can make any decisions.

Resolution – see motion.

Rules of order – a set of rules used to run a meeting. For example, *Bourinot's Rules of Order* or *Robert's Rules of Order* contain instructions on how to make a motion, get the chairs attention, and be respectful.

Supermajority – the percentage of the participants who must approve a special resolution, such as a bylaw change. A supermajority is typically 75 percent or at least 67 percent.

Tabled – the group decides they are not going to decide on the issue at this meeting. The working phrase is "We will table this motion until the next meeting." Typically, this is done when the group wants more time to make the decision.

Appendix A
Policies to Consider

WRITTEN POLICIES ARE the best practice. The organization should take the time to discuss and document the values they want exhibited at the organization's meetings.

Here are some examples of policies that you can choose from. They are just examples . . . Feel free to make your own if these don't fit your organization.

Meeting Administration

What rules do we uses at the meetings?

Effective meetings have rules. There are a couple of possible rules of order the organization can adopt or the organization can develop some of their own rules.

1. We use *Roberts Rules of Order* at our meetings.
2. We use *Bourinot's Rules of Order* at our meetings.
3. We have established our own rules of order.

Can the chair vote?

The group must decide if the chair is going to be allowed to vote or whether the chair will focus on managing the meeting.

1. The chair may only vote in the case of a tie.
2. The chair may not vote on any motion.
3. The chair has a vote on all motions.

Behaviour at the Meeting

If you want well-behaved participants, establish that expectation through setting the appropriate policies.

1. All participants at our meetings will treat each other with respect. Our meetings will focus on the issues not the personalities of the participants.
2. Our meetings will be held in a respectful manner.
3. We will not tolerate a lack of respect from any participant at our meetings.

How does the chair deal with participant behaviour?

Guidelines on the expected behaviour go a long way toward improving meetings. Participants will behave well when they know the expectations.

INTERRUPTIONS

1. Interruptions are only permitted on a point of order, a point of privilege, or by the chair.
2. We have no policy on interruptions.
3. Interrupting a participant who has the floor may be permitted if the interruption is done in a respectful manner.

LATECOMERS

1. All meetings will start on time.
2. All meetings will start within five minutes of the agreed time, unless we don't have quorum.
3. Our meetings will start when we have quorum.
4. Participants who arrive after the meeting is called to order will not be granted entry.
5. Participants who arrive later than five minutes after the appointed time will not be granted entry.
6. Participants who arrive after the meeting is called to order will not be granted entry, unless needed for quorum.

Removal of Board Members

How can the chair remove a participant from a meeting?

Hopefully, participants do not need to be removed from the meeting because of their behaviour, but it is the best practice to have a plan in place, just in case.

1. The chair may ask a participant to leave a meeting if they have been warned about their behaviour twice; the third instance will cause their removal from the meeting.
2. A participant may be removed from the meeting by a motion voted on by secret ballot. The motion may be made by the chair or another participant.
3. A participant may be removed from a meeting at the sole discretion of the chair.

How can the chair remove a participant from the organization?

In the event a participant has become a problem at a meeting, someone/some committee may need to remove the participant from the organization, not just the meeting.

1. If a participant has been asked to leave a meeting, the nominating committee will investigate the behaviour of the board member and make a recommendation to the full board for their removal.

2. The nominating committee may ask a board member to leave the board if they agree there is cause. This removal requires the committee to be unanimous, otherwise the motion goes to the full board and then only a majority is required to pass the motion for removal.
3. Board members may only be removed if they have been warned about their behaviour twice in writing, and the behaviour does not improve. The nominating committee investigates and makes a recommendation, but only the full board in a majority vote can remove a board member from the organization.

Control of the Meeting – Agenda and Quorum

How can items get added to the agenda?

Controlling the addition of items to the agenda ensures that the meeting is a reasonable length and contributes to the organization achieving its goals.

1. Items may only be added to the agenda by board members.
2. Items may only be added to the agenda by the full board.
3. Items may only be added to the agenda by board members and the executive team as a whole.
4. The agenda is circulated prior to the meeting, and

items can be added by any member of the board up to the time when the agenda is finalized. No items may be added to the agenda at the time of the meeting unless the item is an emergency. An emergency is defined as an item that is both urgent and time sensitive. The participants will vote on whether an item can be considered an emergency and can therefore added to the agenda at the last minute.

5. For an item to be added to the agenda at the time of the meeting, the item must be both urgent and crucial – the item needs to be discussed immediately or grave damage will be done to the organization.

What determines quorum?

Meetings cannot do official business without quorum, the number of members needed at the meeting. Different organizations have different number requirements for quorum.

1. Quorum is half of the board plus one. For example, quorum is seven members on a twelve-member board.
2. Quorum is two-thirds of the board. For example, quorum is eight members on a twelve-member board.
3. Quorum is half of the board. For example, quorum is six on a twelve-member board.

How to get the attention of the chair to speak?

Having a rule about only one person at a time being allowed to speak means that participants need a method for getting the attention of the chair without interrupting the current speaker. Of course, if your meetings do not have any rules about interrupting then you won't have policies about how to get the attention of the chair.

1. Participants must raise their hand either in person or virtually to attract the attention of the chair who will nod if the meeting is in person or lower the hand if the meeting is virtual.
2. Participants must make eye contact with the chair who will nod to acknowledge the participant. If the meeting is virtual the participants who wish to speak next will say so in the chat.
3. Participants must pass a note to the chair if the meeting is being held in person or use the chat function if the meeting is being held virtually.

Virtual Meetings

Where can participants attend the meeting from?

The organization should consider how to make the meeting experience equally useful for all participants, whether in person, virtually, or a combination.

1. If the meeting is held virtually, then all

participants will use their own computers to attend the meeting. It is not recommended that a group of participants gather in a meeting room and use one computer to communicate with the other participants.

2. If a meeting is being held in person and less than 10 percent of the participants are attending via virtual meeting software, it is permitted for those in the room to communicate with the others with the one computer in the room.

3. All participants are expected to participate in each meeting whether they are attending in person or virtually.

What virtual meeting tools should the participants use?

There is a trade-off between engagement of the participants and their personal choices.

1. Participants will leave their cameras on during virtual meetings. The chat, screen sharing, and annotation functions will all be available to participants.

2. Participants may leave their cameras on or off at their discretion during virtual meetings. The chat, screen sharing, and annotation functions will all be available to participants.

3. Participants will leave their cameras on during

virtual meetings. The chat, screen sharing, and annotation functions will be disabled.

When does the discussion happen?

Each group can decide at which time the discussion takes place: before or after the motion is made.

1. We make the motion and then have the discussion.
2. We make the motion after the discussion has taken place.
3. We do not have a policy about when the discussion takes place; it can be before or after the motion is made.

How much detail in the minutes?

A board's minutes must contain enough detail that due diligence is demonstrated.

1. The chair will ensure that it is clear from the summary of any discussion that the group demonstrated diligence, followed existing policy, and was transparent.
2. The chair will ensure the ADAPPT board decision-making framework was followed during the meeting.
3. The chair will ensure the minutes of the meeting

capture all the relevant points made during the discussion.

What happens in the case of a tie vote?

Don't wait until your first tie vote to decide how to deal with it.

1. In the event of a tie, the board chair will cast the deciding vote.
2. In the event of a tie, the motion is defeated.
3. In the event of a tie, the motion will be tabled until the next meeting. If the tie persists, then the motion is defeated.

How long and how often are the meetings?

Decide on a meeting length so the participants can make plans for their day.

1. Board meetings may be no longer than three hours.
2. Committee meetings may be no longer than one and a half hours.
3. Board meetings are held on the first Wednesday evening of each month, except for the month of August when there will be no meetings.
4. Board meetings are held every second week on Tuesday morning.

Disclaimer: The information in this book is not intended as personal guidance.

Appendix B
Consolidated List of Things to Do

Which meeting rules should we use?

- ✓ Choose which official rules of order you will use to run your meetings.
- ✓ Write up the key meeting rules that you will remind the participants of at each meeting.

What are the responsibilities of the chair at the meeting?

- ✓ Decide on the goal of the meeting.
- ✓ Create a policy on whether the chair votes.
- ✓ Create policies on what to do when participants are not respectful or are late.
- ✓ Create a policy on how to remove a member from a meeting or from the organization.
- ✓ Create a policy for when additions to the agenda are allowed under both normal and emergency conditions.

- ✓ Make sure you know what quorum is for your organization.
- ✓ Send reminders for meetings and ask for confirmation of attendance to ensure quorum at meetings.
- ✓ Keep track of motions on the floor; make sure the meeting rules are being followed.
- ✓ Create a policy for how participants get the attention of the chair.
- ✓ Keep track of people who would like to speak and call them in order.

How do virtual meetings work?

- ✓ Create policies for the use of video, chat, screen sharing, and annotation in a virtual meeting.
- ✓ Create a policy about how hybrid meetings will work.

When does discussion happen?

- ✓ Create a policy for ensuring the summary of any discussion shows that the group demonstrated diligence, followed existing policy, and was transparent.

How does voting work?

- ✓ Determine the best method for voting on each issue.

Appendix B: Consolidated List of Things to Do

- ✓ Determine what percentage of positive votes is needed for a supermajority and ensure that the conditions requiring a supermajority are known to the board.
- ✓ Create a policy on what should be done in the case of a tie vote.

How do we evaluate the meetings?

- ✓ Set up a way to evaluate the meetings. Determine the questions that need to be asked. Set up a way to keep score over time.
- ✓ Ensure that the board has a way to evaluate the chair.

Other Books by Debi J. Peverill

Basic Board Governance

Budgeting Essentials

Can Your Business be Sold?

Every Canadian's Guide to Financial Prosperity

Painless Financial Literacy

Starting a Successful Business

Ten Tax Traps to Avoid

How to Craft an Effective Agenda

How to Take Minutes Effectively

About the Author

DEBI J. PEVERILL has attended thousands of meetings during her decades-long career as a Chartered Accountant and a professional speaker.

Debi is a rare individual: an accountant with a sense of humour and no fear of public speaking. She has a particular interest in governance, taxation, and financial management.

Debi teaches courses in the Sobeys School of Business at Saint Mary's University, Halifax, runs her public accounting practice, and finds time to record helpful tips on LinkedIn, Twitter, and YouTube twice a week. She also writes on Medium and her own blog at DebiPeverill.ca.

She is the mother of two grown children and lives with her long-suffering husband in Lower Sackville, Nova Scotia.

For More Information

Twitter: @DebiPev

LinkedIn.com/in/DebiPeverill

YouTube.com/c/DebiPeverillPFTG

DebiPev.Medium.com

Peverill.ca (accounting business)
DebiPeverill.ca (financial tips)
PainlessFinancialTrainingGroup.ca (books and courses)

www.ingramcontent.com/pod-product-compliance
Lightning Source LLC
Chambersburg PA
CBHW070347230526
45471CB00006B/2457